WOOLLEN MANUFACTURE.

SHEARING MACHINE.

ABOVE: *A shearing or cropping machine first patented in 1787 consisted of a framework operating two pairs of hand shears. This simple machine was hated and feared by the Huddersfield hand croppers and was the object of attack by Luddite groups in 1812. The rioters used a sledgehammer which they nicknamed 'Enoch' after Enoch and James Taylor, local blacksmiths who made cropping machines. This gave rise to the cry 'Enoch hath made them and Enoch shall break them' as the Luddites smashed the frames.*

COVER: *This semi-automatic mule was made about 1800 and used by Samuel Crompton in his King Street workshop in Bolton until 1815. The headstock placed to one side of the carriage originally drove 220 spindles. Crompton is believed to have owned a similar machine of 360 spindles which was dismantled after his death, the timber being made into a writing desk for his biographer and friend, Gilbert French.*

TEXTILE MACHINES

Anna P. Benson

Shire Publications Ltd

CONTENTS

Set in 9 on 9 point Times roman and printed in Great Britain by C. I. Thomas & Sons (Haverfordwest) Ltd, Press Buildings, Merlins Bridge, Haverfordwest, Dyfed.

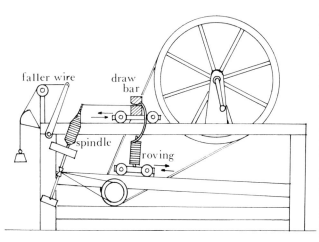

LEFT: *Spinning on an improved jenny. A short length of roving is released through the drawbar, which is then clamped securely. The spinner moves backwards pulling the drawbar carriage out while turning the large flywheel to rotate the spindles. The roving is thus drawn out and one turn of twist is inserted each time it slips off the tip of the rotating spindles. When the carriage is fully drawn the spinner continues to rotate the spindles to insert more twist into the yarn. The spindles are reversed slightly to release the yarn from their tips and the faller wire is brought down to hold the yarn at right angles to the spindles. The spindles are rotated and the carriage is pushed inwards as winding on occurs. The operative is then ready to release another section of roving to start the spinning cycle again.*

RIGHT: *Weaving plain cloth on a power loom. Warp threads are wound on to the warp beam at the back of the loom. Each warp thread passes through an individual eye on a shaft, then through the comb-like reed and finally to the front take-up roller. Alternate warp threads are lifted by the movement of the shafts, while others are depressed to form a V-shaped passage (shed), through which the shuttle carrying the weft thread is propelled. After each weft insertion (pick) the sley which holds the reed moves forward to the position shown in the diagram to beat up the newly inserted weft thread into the body of cloth already woven. The take-up roller turns slightly after each beat up, winding the cloth on to the beam at the front and pulling some more warp from the warp beam at the back.*

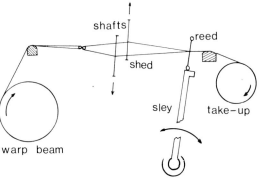

These fulling stocks, now in Leeds Industrial Museum, were made in 1837 by the firm of Pickles of Bramley and used at Moorhead Mills, Gildersome, near Leeds, until 1975.

THE FIRST MACHINES

In medieval times much of England's wealth was based on the annual wool clip, of which a major part was exported to the continent of Europe, where it was made into cloth. Clothmaking in Britain was confined to production for the home market, the main centres of manufacture being corporate towns where guilds held considerable influence.

The introduction of fulling mills in the twelfth century led to a gradual breakdown of the guild monopoly over textile production. *Fulling stocks,* large wooden hammers, operated by tappets replaced the ancient technique of 'walking' or treading repeatedly on wetted cloth to shrink and thicken it, giving woollen fabric its distinctive finish. Stocks required water power to drive the tappet shaft and fulling mills were built at suitable sites, usually in country areas. Small clothmaking centres developed around these new mills.

Domestic textile production was given a further stimulus by the introduction around 1300 of the *spinning wheel,* which put yarn production on a more formal economic basis, eventually ending the casual use of portable drop spindles. The spinning wheel consisted of a spindle driven by a band from a large hand-turned wheel. Spinning was an intermittent process in that two distinct operations were performed: spinning, the drawing out and twisting of fibres to make a yarn; and winding the yarn on to the spindle.

In contrast, the introduction of the *bobbin and flyer wheel,* in the fifteenth century, allowed continuous spinning. The twist was inserted into the drawn-out fibres by a horseshoe-shaped flyer and the rotation of one large and one small pulley by a double drive band enabled

ABOVE: *A domestic interior showing spinning on a great wheel, from Walker's 'Costume of Yorkshire' (1814).*

LEFT: *The first known illustration of a bobbin and flyer wheel, from the medieval house book of 1480. This intriguing piece of evidence shows a type of wheel which until recently was not thought to have existed until 1530. The text in the manuscript is unrevealing, as it does not directly refer to the illustration.*

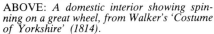

the bobbin and flyer to turn at different speeds, causing the yarn to wind on automatically. This wheel, known as the *Saxony* or *flax wheel,* could double the production of the ordinary or *great wheel* but was generally limited to producing strong yarns made from long fibres such as flax and longer wools because of the considerable tension applied to the fibres during spinning. Woollen, cotton and other short fibre yarns continued to be produced on the great wheel until the introduction of machine spinning in the eighteenth century.

Weaving, the interlacing of two sets of threads, the warp and the weft, to create fabric was performed on vertical warp-

ABOVE: *An unusual photograph showing Queen Victoria spinning flax on a Saxony wheel. The widespread introduction of machine spinning brought the end of the domestic system, making the production of home spun yarn unnecessary. From being a laborious but essential task for most women, hand spinning became a fashionable drawing-room pastime.*

BELOW: *A simple two-treadle horizontal handloom of about 1500. By depressing one treadle with her foot, the weaver brings down half the warp threads producing a V-shaped passage or shed through which the shuttle carrying the weft thread is thrown. She beats up the weft to the edge or fell of the cloth already woven, using the batten or sley which hangs vertically from a separate top frame.*

A model of a nineteenth-century Coventry ribbon loom incorporating a Jacquard selection mechanism and a rack and pinion shuttle device. The shuttles carrying the weft threads are moved from side to side by the toothed wheels geared into a rack operated by a 'marionette', seen on the left. This rack and pinion method, developed by Vaucanson, superseded a simple driving system using pegs which pushed the shuttle through the warp.

The teasel gig mill was developed in the sixteenth century to raise the nap on woollen cloth but its use was forbidden by an Act of Parliament in order to protect the jobs of hand raisers.

weighted looms until about 1300, when *horizontal looms* came into widespread use. This enabled a number of warp threads to be lifted by the operation of treadles, making a V-shaped passage (the shed) through which a shuttle carrying the weft thread was propelled.

During the sixteenth century Walloon immigrants introduced many new fabrics such as worsted stuffs and cotton mix cloths. Broad looms came into greater use to create the wider fabrics popular on the European mainland but these looms required two weavers to throw the shuttle from side to side.

Narrow fabrics or tapes were produced on the newly introduced Dutch *ribbon loom*. A number of tapes could be woven simultaneously as a series of tiny shuttles were actuated by a peg or driver to carry the weft threads across a number of individual warps.

The establishment of a textile production system based on hand techniques engendered resistance to the introduction of machines, a theme which recurs throughout the history of textiles. Although fulling stocks were accepted in the domestic system there was organised resistance to the *gig mill*. This machine consisted of battens mounted with teasels (a type of thistle) fixed on a cylinder which rotated against woollen cloth, performing a brushing action, thereby raising the surface fibres (the nap). Gig mills were reintroduced about 1800 and suffered at the hands of machine breakers but they were eventually accepted later in the nineteenth century.

ABOVE: *A nineteenth-century Scottish handloom with dobby attachment showing a drop box mechanism and fly shuttle device. The method of lifting the boxes and the curved springs which return the picker are peculiar to Scottish and Scandinavian handlooms.*

BELOW: *Automatic take-up motions were introduced in the eighteenth century in an attempt to make hand weaving more efficient. Each time the weaver moved the sley to beat up the weft the ratchet and pawl shown in the illustration turned the cloth roller. Cast iron hand looms incorporating automatic take-up motions were known as dandy looms.*

An eighteenth-century wool carding engine in a reconstructed woollen mill at Old Sturbridge Village, Massachusetts, USA. The operative is removing the fibres from the doffer in a number of individual lengths. These would be pieced together, drawn out, and lightly twisted on a slubbing billy before being made into yarn on a spinning jenny.

THE EXPANSION OF THE DOMESTIC SYSTEM

In the eighteenth century the close inter-dependence of textiles and agriculture began to break down. Spinners and weavers were often wholly employed in their occupations by wealthy merchants who bought stocks of fibre or yarn and put out these raw materials to weavers who were paid a set amount per woven piece. The decline of the independent weaver was part of a move towards greater organisation, with capitalist clothiers controlling production, often with as many as two thousand outwork-ers. Some clothiers set up small work-shops known as loomshops in an attempt to centralise textile production.

In 1733 John Kay patented the *fly shuttle device,* an amazingly simple idea, which enabled the weaver to sit centrally at the loom and propel the shuttle through the warp from side to side by pulling buffers or pickers along a slide-rod in a box fixed to each end of the sley.[1] By combining this idea with a wheeled shuttle, broad cloth (over 36 inches, 914 mm, wide) could be woven by one weaver instead of two. The fly shuttle device was first used in woollen manufac-turing areas north of Bury, where Kay took legal action against weavers who had modified their looms in defiance of his patent.

In 1760 John Kay's son Robert devised sets of boxes which moved up and down to allow one of three shuttles to be fired across the warp, providing a weft striping capacity, and this achieved a more widespread use of the fly shuttle device.

The carding process to disentangle and straighten the fibres was improved in a similar way. Old hand cards were replaced by the stock card, in which one hand card was used in conjunction with a table covered with card clothing (bent wire pins), allowing more fibre to be processed.

Rotary *carding engines* were patented separately by Lewis Paul and Daniel Bourne in 1748. One of Bourne's engines was acquired by the Peels, the famous manufacturing family, but was set aside as being unprofitable. The problem with these engines was the absence of a motion to remove the carded fibres. It was necessary for an operative to stand at the delivery end of the carding engine and periodically strip the fibres from the final roller or doffer with a needle stick. Nevertheless in the woollen industry this type of engine was used long after the introduction of continuous carding in 1775. Rotary cards were easily incorporated into existing fulling mills, which in their enlarged form were known as scribbling mills and formed the basis for the development of vertical woollen mills (all processes under one roof).

Greater efficiency in fibre preparation and weaving, emphasised by the increase in potential markets, put pressure on spinners and led Edward Baines, the historian, to observe: 'The one thread wheel, though turning from morning till night in thousands of cottages, could not keep pace with the weaver's shuttle or with the demands of the merchant.' The resulting yarn shortage generated the invention of numerous multi-spindle spinning wheels, few of which proved successful. A significant attempt was made by Lewis Paul and his mechanic John Wyatt in a patent of 1738, which embodied the idea of roller drafting by substituting sets of rollers for the spinner's fingers. 'A succession of . . . rowlers, cillinders or cones moving proportionately faster' drew out the roving to a predetermined thickness ready for twisting. However this idea was not exploited and the inventors de-

A slubbing billy, which pieced together and lightly twisted the short ropes of fibres produced on the carding engine. These continuous lengths, now called slubbing, were then ready for spinning on the jenny or mule. The billy was eventually superseded by the piecing machine, invented in America in 1826.

ABOVE LEFT: *Releasing a portion of slubbing through the clamp or drawbar on an improved spinning jenny.*

ABOVE RIGHT: *The clamp is firmly shut and the operative carefully draws back the carriage while turning the large drive wheel which turns the spindles. One turn of twist is inserted into the yarn each time it slips off the tip of the spindle. When a full length of slubbing has been drawn out more twist is inserted to make a strong yarn which has to be wound on to the spindles before another section of slubbing can be spun.*

RIGHT: *Winding on is performed by presenting the yarn at right angles to the spindles by bringing down a faller wire controlled by a lever on the drawbar. The operative turns the drive wheel and pushes the carriage inwards while guiding the yarn on to the spindles to form a cop.*

veloped another scheme, that of drawing out the roving and twisting between one set of rollers and a rotating spindle. This is not a workable concept as it would mean drawing out or drafting against a substantial amount of twist. They failed to appreciate the relationship between drafting and twisting and the mills they established did not prosper.

It was 1764 before a successful multi-spindle machine was invented by James Hargreaves, a cotton weaver from Oswaldtwistle, Lancashire. The *jenny,* meaning 'engine', was developed on the great wheel principle of drafting and twisting in one stage and winding on to the spindle in another.

Hargreaves made a number of jennies for Lancashire spinners, then moved to Nottingham in 1768 and set up a jenny factory. He did not patent his idea until 1770 and yet the machine illustrated in the patent drawing retains some awkward features. The faller wire, used to change the angle of presentation of yarn to the spindle for winding on, was foot controlled and the drive wheel set almost horizontal, making it difficult to turn. Tests on reproduction jennies constructed from the patent drawing demonstrate that spinning on these early machines required great skill. The jenny was subsequently altered and improved to incorpo-rate a vertical drive wheel, a moving carriage on wheels and a hand-operated faller wire. The most significant change was the introduction of a long tin roller to equalise the drive to the spindles.

Spinning trials on an improved jenny prove that it is difficult to create a consistent hard twist yarn of the type required for framework knitting or for the warp in weaving. Perhaps this was why Hargreaves and his partner, Thomas James, relinquished the production of jenny yarn in favour of Arkwright's system, which produced a yarn more suitable for the Nottingham knitting industry.

In Lancashire, however, the soft and lofty jenny yarn was in great demand as weft for weaving and jennies were made in their thousands by local joiners. The intermittent action of these machines was not readily suited to the application of power. Many were eventually used in jenny shops and factories but smaller jennies were ideal for domestic operation and took the place of the great wheel in the home.

Initially used for cotton, jennies were adapted for woollen spinning, a process for which they were eminently suited. In this form the woollen jenny propped up a declining domestic system well into the nineteenth century.

The lantern frame, so called because the cans at the front resembled lanterns, was invented by Arkwright to produce roving for his water frame. Sliver from the draw frame was fed through drafting rollers and lightly twisted between these and nip rollers fixed to the top of the rotating can. After twisting, the roving was taken inside the can and later hand-wound on to bobbins.

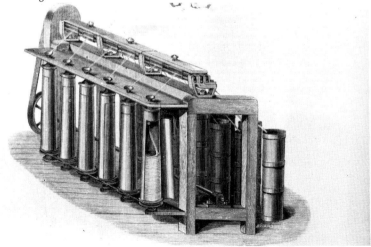

Some original Cromford machines which can be seen at Higher Mill Museum, Helmshore. In the foreground are the hand and powered lap formers which provide the feed for the carding engines in the background.

THE FACTORY SYSTEM

The invention of the spinning machine which became known as the *water frame* inaugurated a new style of textile production called the factory system. This machine might well have remained a domestic hand-operated device like the jenny but for the vision and will power of its inventor, Richard Arkwright, who extended and developed it into an industrial machine.

The prototype spinning machine was patented in 1769 and could spin four threads at once, using drafting rollers and the flyer type of continuous spinning performed by the Saxony wheel, a process particularly suited to the application of power.

The search for a constant reliable source of power led Arkwright to set up his first water-powered mill in Cromford, Derbyshire, in 1771. He also realised that his spinning frames would fail if the input material (roving) still had to be spun by hand on the great wheel. Thus his second patent of 1775 encompasses a variety of preparatory machines to serve the water frame.

Carding engines existed before 1775 but Arkwright sought to achieve a continuous process by adding a constant feed in the form of a roll of canvas containing a sheet of fibres and a constant output by means of a crank and comb, a neat stripping device which removed the fibres in web form and fed them into rollers which compressed the cotton into a long rope of untwisted fibres called sliver. The roll of canvas was later abandoned as Arkwright discovered that a wad of cotton did not need reinforcement and so a machine to form laps was developed. The invention of a powered *lap former* has been credited to Arkwright's son, Richard.

The sliver from the carding engine was transferred to the *draw frame,* where it was attenuated by drafting rollers and combined with sliver from three other cards to form one sliver relatively free of irregularities. This was an essential stage in the production of an even yarn as the continuous nature of spinning on the water frame meant that the final thread was only as regular as the roving fed in, in

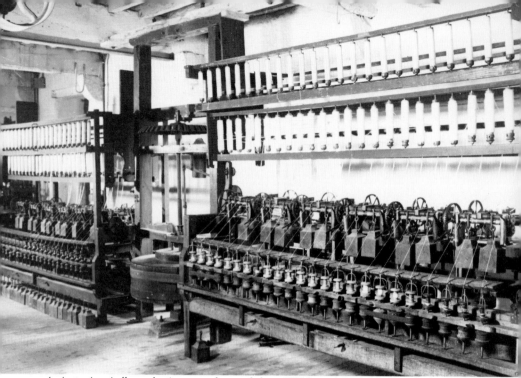

A ninety-six spindle production water frame of about 1785 from Arkwright's Cromford mill. Power from a waterwheel was transmitted via shafting to the bevel gear at the top of the central headstock and the large drum at the base carried drive belts to each side of the frame. It was this type of machine which determined the width of early spinning mills as water frames were placed across the mill with the drive shaft running lengthways through their centres. The addition of a gangway at the side of the frames meant that the mills were usually built about 30 feet (9 m) wide.

contrast with the later mule, which could even out irregularities in poor roving. Whenever the water frame seemed to be producing uneven yarn Arkwright would tell his operatives to 'look to your drawings', in other words to go back to the draw frame to ensure good quality sliver was being produced.

The *lantern frame* converted sliver into roving, a lightly twisted rope of fibres sufficiently strong for use on the water frame. At this point there occurs a break in continuity, as the roving could not be wound on to a bobbin owing to the absence of a winding mechanism. It is possible that Arkwright tried to wind roving on to bobbins by the method used on the water frame, which relied on the flyer and yarn to rotate the bobbin. However, roving is not strong enough to withstand the frictional resistance of the bobbin and would break under the strain. The roving was therefore allowed to coil up inside the lanterns and children were employed to rewind it on to bobbins, which were then fixed to the creel above the water frame. From the creel the roving was fed through sets of drafting rollers, the front pair rotating faster than the back pair, thus drawing out the roving while the flyer rotated twisting the attenuated roving.

The positioning of the rollers relative to the staple length of the fibre being processed was critical to successful spinning, a fact not fully appreciated by Wyatt and Paul, who introduced the idea of roller drafting in 1738.

Arkwright employed clockmakers to fashion the gear mechanism. The gear wheels on the water frame, the largest being 6 inches (152 mm) in diameter, were cut out of solid brass. Because of the malleable nature of brass, Arkwright had to design the water frame as a compounding of individual heads containing four spindles and flyers and two sets of drafting rollers, each with individual gearing and a dog clutch mechanism. Later technology allowed relatively fine iron gears to be cast and the introduction of the tin roller spindle drive led to the first development of the water frame, the *throstle*.

Multiples of each machine were made, all driven by water power and housed under one roof. While he held patent rights Arkwright exercised absolute control over the use of his system, allowing people to manufacture under licence, but only those willing to pay for the whole series of machines. It was therefore necessary for anyone using his system to have a purpose-built mill with a power source and plenty of initial capital.

Factories modelled on the Arkwright system became established throughout Britain, some in defiance of his patent rights. Many manufacturers bitterly resented the control exercised by Arkwright over his system. At the same time social unrest caused the new mills to become targets for machine breakers, including one rented by Arkwright at Birkacre near Chorley, Lancashire, in 1779. This particular event persuaded Samuel Crompton, living near Bolton, to dismantle and temporarily hide a new spinning machine he had recently developed.

Crompton was a weaver of fustians (cloth with a linen warp and a cotton weft), who used an eight-spindle jenny to spin his own cotton yarn. Because of the demand for lightweight cotton goods he attempted to use his jenny to create fine hard twist yarns suitable for warps, but without success. Only one spun length in ten was satisfactory. The machine he developed to improve the jenny became known as the *mule* as it combined the bare spindle spinning of the jenny with the drafting rollers of the water frame. It is, however, a development of the great wheel or jenny system of intermittent spinning.

During the creation of the first mule Crompton experimented with one pair of drafting rollers, assuming like others before him that roving would attenuate itself when taken through the nip of two rollers (one on top of the other). Realis-

ing that one pair of rollers could not draft, he developed the delivery to incorporate two pairs of drafting rollers. In addition he used the jenny method of drafting by arranging for the spindles fixed to a carriage on tracks to move out at a slightly faster rate than the roving was delivered. This carriage draft gave an extra stretch to the yarn and dispersed any irregularities.

The mule was also known as the muslin wheel as it was capable of spinning very fine cotton yarns suitable for weaving into lightweight cotton cloth. There was such a demand for this superior yarn that Crompton was at first able to command a price of 25 shillings per pound (0.45 kg) for 60s count (i.e. 60 by 840 yards per pound) and 42 shillings for the extremely fine 80s count yarn.

Crompton's mule was never patented, apparently on the advice of a local manufacturer, Pilkington, who had witnessed the stagnating effect of Arkwright's patents on the ordinary

The action of a water frame. Roving is fed through the drafting rollers from left to right in the diagram and is attenuated in the zone between the back roller and the faster front roller. The drawn-out roving is delivered from the front roller and immediately twisted by the action of the flyer. Each time the flyer rotates, one turn of twist is inserted into the drawn-out roving and the resultant yarn is wound on to the bobbin.

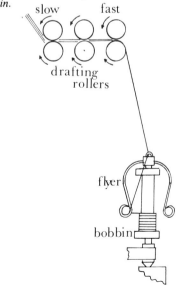

slow   fast

drafting rollers

flyer

bobbin

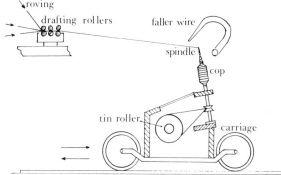

The spinning cycle of a self-acting mule. Roving is fed through drafting rollers as the carriage moves outwards. At the same time the spindles rotate, inserting one turn of twist into the drawn-out roving at each rotation. When the carriage reaches the full extent of its draw the drafting rollers and carriage stop but the spindles continue to rotate rapidly, to put more twist into the yarn. The spindles then stop, rotate backwards slightly to take the yarn off the tips of the spindles and the faller wire comes down and holds the yarn at right angles to the spindles for winding on. The spindles rotate more slowly than before and the length of yarn just spun is wound on to the spindles as the carriage moves inwards. On completion of the winding-on process the cycle starts again.

manufacturer. For a derisory reward Crompton released all the construction details of his mule. This ingenious machine was of crude timber construction, with a system of pulleys and bands to drive the drafting rollers and spindles. The original fluted drafting rollers (the lower ones) were also of wood, into which Crompton inserted lengths of wire in order to prevent slippage during drafting, and the spindles were adapted from flax hackles, large metal combs used in the preparation of linen yarn.

Improvements were made to the first mules almost at once. A mule used by Crompton in his King Street workshop shows the addition of Henry Stone's fluted metal rollers and William Kelly's gearing. Other developments include centralised headstocks, leading to their use in pairs. The records of Dobson and Rothwell (later Dobson and Barlow) show orders for pairs in 1798. The mule required highly skilled labour even when it was made semi-automatic, and there was a limit to the number of spindles which could be operated by one man.

Because he did not patent the mule, Crompton was never fully rewarded for inventing it. But during his lifetime it was transformed from a small domestic device into a factory machine with many hundreds of spindles.

Two further inventions completed the mechanisation of the spinning process from raw cotton to spun yarn. The first

was an American development to remove seeds from cotton fibres, a process known as ginning. Eli Whitney's *cotton gin* of 1793 was the forerunner of the saw gin and was a rotating cylinder fixed with hooks which protruded through slots, catching the cotton fibres and leaving the seeds behind. The gin was operated by horse power and could do the work of fifty slaves using hand gins. Whitney's gin revitalised the plantations, vastly increasing the amount of raw cotton available for export, and this found a ready market in the rapidly developing textile industry of Great Britain.

Further cleaning to remove dirt and trash was carried out when the ginned cotton arrived in Britain. Women beat the cotton with willow sticks, causing the dirt to fall through a mesh. Arkwright type mills relied on outworkers to perform this task, which was known as batting. The invention of the *scutcher* by Neil Snodgrass of Glasgow in 1797 mechanised this hand process. This scutcher, which was never patented and of which no record survives, was rather like a threshing machine with revolving beaters. Its action was drastic, so high quality cottons were batted by hand well into the nineteenth century.

The rapid advance in spinning technology created a need for the mechanisation of weaving. The Reverend Edmund Cartwright's first power loom was patented in 1785 and was developed in total ignor-

ABOVE: *This semi-automatic or hand mule made by John Davies, a well known millwright from Montgomeryshire (now part of Powys), is not a true mule as it does not draft the fibres by rollers but relies on a small amount of spindle draft caused by the carriage being moved outwards after the rollers have ceased to deliver slubbing.*

BELOW: *A model of Edmund Cartwright's second power loom. Warp threads were taken from bobbins mounted on a free-standing creel at the back of the loom, through a size box and around tensioning rollers. The warp passed in a conventional manner through two shafts and a reed to separate the threads, and the woven cloth collected in a box.*

ance of handloom weaving, a process he decided to investigate only after he applied for a patent. He discovered that the handloom produced cloth with ease and simplicity whereas his loom, with a vertical warp and spring-operated beat up, needed two strong men to operate it even for short periods. His second patent of 1786 was over-elaborate, incorporating a warping mechanism and an automatic device for sizing. (Size is a starch mixture applied to reinforce the warp during weaving.) Despite its complexity, this loom contained the elements used on future successful looms. Cartwright introduced a set of revolving cams to operate the picking and shedding motions and the sley. A worm drive controlled both the let-off and take-up motions, and an attempt was made to stop the loom if either a warp or weft thread broke. Cartwright persisted in developing three further patent machines and invested £30,000 in a steam-powered weaving mill in Doncaster. This venture failed but Cartwright's ingenuity was recognised by Parliament, which voted him £10,000 compensation in 1808.

The ancient craft of printing was converted from hand to machine operation at this time. The *cylinder printing machine* was patented by Thomas Bell in 1783 and could print six colours on to a plain cotton cloth by means of engraved copper rollers. Each roller was coated with dye paste from a separate bowl and a 'doctor blade' removed excess paste before printing, leaving the dye in the engraved areas. The cloth passed over the six rollers, receiving the multi-coloured design.

The advance of the factory system was accelerated by the development of a new power source, the stationary steam engine. In 1785 the first rotative beam engine was applied to a cotton mill. Henceforth textile mills no longer had to be sited in rural areas where water power was available, for steam allowed the establishment of factories in urban areas, and so the mill towns grew.

Flax spreading and hackling machines in York Street Mill, Belfast, about 1900. Hackling is a combing process which straightens the long flax fibres known as line and removes the shorter fibres called tow. One of the principal suppliers of flax processing equipment is the firm of James Mackie and Sons, which was founded in 1846 to make components for the flax industry but within a few years was providing a complete range of machinery for the rapidly expanding linen industry of Northern Ireland. The firm has also increased its range to include equipment for extruding and processing polypropylene and other synthetic fibres.

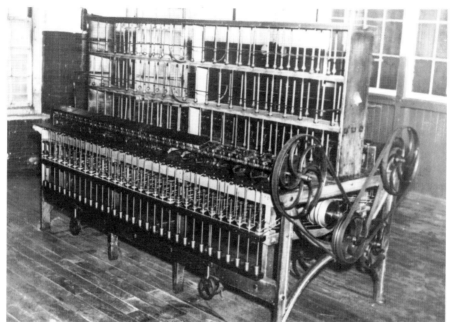

A sixty-four spindle throstle spinning machine used by the Merrimack Company, Lowell, Massachusetts, in 1830. The name 'throstle' was given to these machines because a number of them operating together would produce a high-pitched singing noise reminiscent of the song of the throstle or song thrush. The main drive transmitted power to the spindles by means of a tin roller, the end of which can be seen in the photograph.

THE AGE OF THE MACHINERY MAKERS

The establishment of the factory system led to the development of specialist textile machinery makers. The first factory masters employed blacksmiths, joiners and clockmakers to make prototype machines. Apprenticed to these mill-based mechanics was a generation of specially trained textile engineers with a sound knowledge of the requirements of textile processing.

One of these apprentices, Samuel Slater, who learned his trade in Jedediah Strutt's mill at Belper, Derbyshire, emigrated to America in 1789 and founded the factory system in Pawtucket, Rhode Island, using his considerable knowledge of Arkwright machines, which he reproduced from memory. In the United States, textile machinery makers re-mained mill based, working in machine shops housed in the basement of mills. One of the largest textile engineering firms, the Whitin Machine Shop, was founded in the basement of the North-bridge Cotton Manufacturing Company in 1809.

In Britain textile machinery making developed in two ways. The new generation of textile mechanics often established their own businesses making and selling components and machines. William Smith, founder of the worsted machinery firm of Prince Smith and Son, was originally apprenticed to a firm of cotton spinners as a mechanic, but he later established a business as a clock-maker in two tiny cottages in Waggon Fold (now Market Street), Keighley,

West Yorkshire, making metal parts such as gears and spindles. In 1800 he embarked on a career of making complete machines, the first a wooden-framed throstle, which was a development of the water frame. The spindles and rollers were driven from one set of gears placed at the end of the machine and known as the headstock, replacing the sets of brass gears serving individual heads on the water frame. The tin roller, so successfully used on the jenny and mule to increase spindle capacity, was incorporated into the throstle.

Other firms which grew to pre-eminence in the industrial age began in even more humble circumstances. Henry Platt was the village blacksmith in Dobcross, a rural village, now in Greater Manchester but then in Yorkshire, and making farm tools and shoeing horses were as important a part of his business as making jennies and card cylinders. As the woollen industry grew in Yorkshire, the need for textile machines increased and Henry Platt enlarged his premises at Bridge House to meet this need. This was the foundation of the firm of Platts, which was to employ twelve thousand people, two thousand of them in coal mines, at the beginning of the twentieth century but which in 1770 was a family business selling eight-spindle common jennies for 18 shillings each.

In 1821, Platts moved to Ferney Bank, Oldham, where they established a foundry, reflecting the increasing use of cast iron. Machines for cutting brass gears had been used by some clockmakers in the eighteenth century but *Rees Cyclopaedia* wrote in about 1810: 'Mr George Gilpin of Sheffield has invented a method of cutting wheels from solid cast iron, with as much accuracy and as good a finish as brass wheels have hitherto been cut, making a very great saving in the expense of brass for a large mill and much more durable when done.'

Improved cast iron throstle speeds were limited to 4000 rpm and its eventual successor, the *ring frame,* did little better until improvements to bearings and spindles were made later in the century. Ring spinning, a development on the continuous principle, was invented by John Thorpe of Providence, Rhode Island, and was improved as the *ring and traveller* in 1829. The ring and traveller replaced the need for a heavy flyer to rotate with the spindle as on the throstle and water frame. A ring fixed at the base of the spindle carried a freely rotating wire hook called a traveller, through which the yarn ran, receiving one turn of twist at every rotation. As the spindle rotated, the yarn ballooned out, causing an air drag, which slowed down the traveller sufficiently to create a difference in speed betweeen spindle and traveller, facilitating automatic winding on. Ring spinning was popular in the United States but the intermittent system exemplified by the mule was favoured by British manufacturers. The semi-powered mule or mule-jenny required an extremely skilled operative with a good deal of physical strength to push the carriage back while controlling the winding-on sequence manually.

A spate of self-actors was patented between 1800 and 1830 but none of these overcame the problem of winding on and cop building, and they were therefore not successful. Richard Roberts, a Welsh millwright working in Manchester, was approached by a group of millowners after a major spinners' strike and persuaded to develop a completely self-acting mule. In 1825 he patented a winding operation, independent of the main drive, which created the cigar-shaped cop of yarn for immediate use in the shuttle. He perfected the self-actor in 1830 by inventing the quadrant, which directly linked carriage movement inwards with spindle rotation so that as the diameter of the cop increased the number of revolutions of the spindles in relation to movement of the carriage decreased.

Roberts's automatic mule was an immediate success although it was used only for coarser yarns at first, finer counts still being spun on mule-jennies. Over one thousand patents relating to spinning mules have been taken out since 1830, but most have been concerned with refining the basic mule invented by Samuel Crompton and perfected by Richard Roberts.

There were numerous significant improvements made to Cartwright's original power loom, most of which retained the

ABOVE: *Ring spinning was developed in America in 1828 but was not immediately popular in Britain. This machine, built by James Sykes of Huddersfield in about 1865, was installed in Peter Anderson's Bridge Mill in Galashiels, where it was used until 1968. Ring spinning is a continuous process which normally produces a strong but lean yarn not generally favoured by woollen manufacturers, who require a full and lofty yarn. It is therefore unusual to find such an early machine surviving, as even those manufacturers who tried ring spinning usually reverted back to mules, which could provide the type of yarn they required.*

BELOW: *A cotton mule on the Platts stand at the London Exhibition of 1862. The American Civil War of 1861 led to a famine in cotton supplies to Britain and many textile machinery firms and manufacturers went out of business. John Platt showed initiative by converting his range of textile machines to process shorter staple cottons from India.*

An early type of power loom used in a remote Welsh woollen mill until the Second World War. The loom has a cast iron frame but its evolution from the handloom can be seen in the wooden sley and the one central picking motion, which is a mechanical version of the fly shuttle device.

wooden framing of the handloom. In 1796 Robert Miller of Glasgow introduced the *wiper loom,* in which the lifting of warp threads (shedding) was actuated by rotating cams, or wipers, and William Horrocks of Stockport developed cranks to operate the beating-up action of the sley and controlled shedding by installing a separate tappet shaft. Again it was Richard Roberts who combined the best aspects of power loom patents and amalgamated a number of ideas with the available technology to produce in 1822 a power loom with a cast iron frame and capable of mass production.

These early tappet or wiper looms were suitable for weaving only relatively plain cloth. Complex weaves and fancy checks were produced on handlooms even after the inventions of the *Jacquard* (1801) and the *dobby* (1824). These selection mechanisms were placed on top of the handloom frame. The Jacquard could be programmed to lift any warp thread independently of any other in a section of warp, giving wide scope for patterning in the production of cloth such as silk brocade. The dobby worked on a similar principle but lifted shafts carrying a number of warp threads and was therefore suited to small geometric designs.

These two devices were eventually adapted to the power loom but their method of lifting threads limited running speeds, so the handloom remained the most common method of making fancy cloth until the invention of the double lift dobby in 1867 by Hattersley and Smith. This mechanism increased fancy loom speeds in line with plain tappet looms, operating at over two hundred picks per minute (four shoots of weft per second).

George Hattersley and Sons, founded in 1789, were originally spindle manufacturers but became famous for their looms and weaving equipment. In 1834, they were the first to make a loom specifically for the worsted industry, but it was destroyed at Nabwood, near Shipley, West Yorkshire, by a riotous mob of

A model loom in the Musée des Tissus, Lyon, France, showing Joseph Marie Jacquard's original selection device of 1801, which was based on the looms of Bouchon and Vaucanson. The mechanism contains a set of hooks linked via a system of cords to the warp threads. A chain of punched cards laced together programmes needles which deflect selected hooks into the path of a rising knife to lift a number of warp threads. Any needle can be programmed independently of any other by punching a hole for a lift, leaving a blank for a thread to stay down. In France there was a great deal of opposition to the introduction of Jacquard's machine but it was immediately successful in Britain. Specialist firms such as Devoges of Manchester and Dracup of Bradford have been responsible for producing Jacquards for many loom manufacturers. The number of needles in the mechanism differs from area to area, Lancashire and Huddersfield usually having four hundred, Bradford three hundred and Belfast and some European silk areas as many as eighteen hundred for greater patterning capacity.

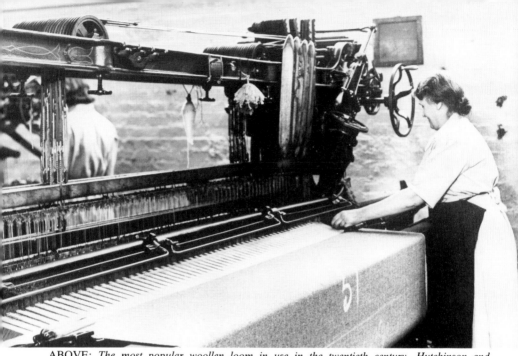

ABOVE: *The most popular woollen loom in use in the twentieth century. Hutchinson and Hollingworth's Dobcross loom, which took its name from its place of manufacture, can be found in the woollen mills of Wales, Yorkshire and Scotland. It is fitted with a dobby mechanism which allows fancy patterns to be woven.*

BELOW: *The woollen industry developed slowly as the early cotton and worsted spinning machines were not easily adapted for the production of woollen yarns. Wool goes through very few processes to be made into yarn. The most important, carding, takes place on an extensive machine made up of a number of roller cards. A thorough cleaning, disentangling, mixing and blending of fibres takes place before the condenser produces wound bobbins of slubbing, created between leather rubbers, which are ready to be spun.*

A Noble comb in William Fison's Greenholme Mills, Bradford, in 1904. The Noble comb has one large circular comb of pins containing two smaller circular combs which rotate in a clockwise direction. The balls of wool sliver are placed around the circumference of the machine and introduced into the combs by feed boxes where the large and small combs meet. The fibres are pushed into the pins of each moving circle by dabbing brushes and both combs take part of the wool. As the circles diverge the fibres are gradually combed and separated. The longer ones are drawn off through drawing rollers and combined to form 'top', which coils into a can at the side of the machine. The shorter fibres (noil) remain in the pins of the smaller circles and are removed by noil knives. Noil, the waste product of worsted production, forms a useful raw material for the woollen industry.

workpeople who opposed its introduction, blaming the power loom for taking work from the handloom weaver.

The Luddite actions of 1811, the power loom riots of 1826, and numerous smaller outrages did little to halt the progress of textile machine development. The immense growth of some textile engineering firms is shown by an advertisement which appeared in the *Bolton Free Press* in 1846 for the sale of equipment at Dobson and Barlow as the firm was moving to larger premises: 'several large machine shops, iron and brass foundries, smithies, saw pit, stove, iron warehouses, joiner's shop, timber yard – also the mill gearing, lathes, planing machine, slotting machine, wheel cutting machine, slide lathes, drilling engines, boring machines and a stock of patterns.'

At the height of the railway age in 1854 Platt Brothers was the largest engineering firm in the world, a position it held until relatively recent times. Platts calico looms were produced at a rate of three hundred a week and sold at £10 15s for a 36 inch (914 mm) weaving width.

Worsted yarn is usually made from long fibres which are parallelised before spinning by combing and drafting processes. Hand combing was an extremely skilled job in which the woolcomber performed a lashing action with one heated wool comb upon another fixed comb holding the fibres. In this way the long wools were separated from the short (noil) and formed into 'top', a length of combed parallel fibres ready for spinning. Although the water frame was quickly adapted to worsted spinning by increasing the distance between drafting rollers and changing gear ratios, combing remained a hand process well into the nineteenth century despite early attempts at mechanisation.

Edmund Cartwright, the inventor of the power loom, in 1790 and 1792 patented combing machines known as 'Big Ben'. These machines attempted to copy the hand action with a device called a crank lasher, but as the input material had to be hand-combed first it was never particularly successful. The mechanisation of this intricate hand process was achieved in a series of successful combs by Donisthorpe and Lister in 1850, and finally, in 1853, by James Noble, whose machines became widely adopted, forming the basis of the Bradford system of worsted spinning.

The immense growth of textile machinery making in Britain in the early nineteenth century was entirely to satisfy a home market. The export of textile machinery was forbidden by statute, but an Order in Council in 1843 revoked this law and opened the way for expansion of the textile industry worldwide. The Great Exhibition of 1851 was the expression of this expansionist period, and by the end of the nineteenth century almost every industrial nation had a textile industry based on British machinery.

After the opening of the Manchester Ship Canal in 1894, Platts loaded steamers at Salford Docks with their machinery made at Oldham, to be unloaded first at Finlays' mills in Bombay and Calcutta and then on to Nagasaki, Japan, where they had a virtual monopoly of textile machinery imports.

At this time a typical power loom achieved high speeds but low efficiency as the machine stopped each time the weaver had to replace manually a full weft pirn in the shuttle. The invention of the *Northrop*, the first system to replace the weft automatically without stopping the loom, was probably the highest stage of mechanisation of traditional handloom techniques. A rotating battery of twenty-four pirns was positioned on the right-hand side of a Northrop loom. On the opposite side a feeler motion touched the pirn each time the shuttle entered the box. When the yarn was almost exhausted the feeler activated a lever which ensured that once the shuttle reached the right-hand box a powerful transfer hammer ejected the spent pirn, replacing it with a full one.

Normally only one battery was fitted, making the loom suitable for plain cloth production. The British textile industry specialised in a variety of fancy fabrics and did not welcome the Northrop sys-

The British export drive was so fierce that in the late nineteenth century some markets were almost saturated, leading to a wider search for potential customers. In 1890 Hattersley and Sons of Keighley developed their famous 'domestic', a treadle-operated power loom (technically classed as a handloom) for underdeveloped countries, where a source of power was not readily available. The Hattersley domestic eventually became associated with the Scottish tweed industry and is still used by the weavers of the Isle of Lewis for creating hand-woven Harris tweed.

An early 'A' model Northrop automatic power loom manufactured in America in 1895. James Northrop, a Yorkshireman who worked for George Draper and Sons of Hopedale, Massachusetts, invented the first device to replenish the weft in the shuttle without stopping the loom. As well as the distinctive rotating battery of weft pirns, the loom incorporated warp and weft stop motions patented by Drapers' Charles Roper, these being essential to the success of an automatic loom. The first Northrops were installed in 1894 when 792 looms were sold to Queen City cotton mills in Burlington, Vermont, where one weaver ran sixteen looms instead of four.

tem. In 1930 95 per cent of all American looms were automatic compared with only 5 per cent in Britain.

The Northrop consisted of standardised parts whereas most British machines were produced in hundreds of variants as models were updated regularly. At Prince Smith and Sons, of Keighley, ideas for new machines were drawn in chalk on the floor in the blacksmithing tradition and in this form ideas would be transmitted to the pattern maker. The introduction of drawing offices to the major textile machinery makers at the beginning of the twentieth century did little towards standardising machines and British firms began to lose business partly because of the difficulty in obtaining spare parts for older machines. Hattersleys attempted to standardise the tradi-

tional loom so that parts from different models were interchangeable, resulting in the Hattersley standard loom, a popular machine which can still be seen operating in a number of woollen mills in Britain.

The heyday of British textile engineering was the period before the First World War when machines were being exported all over the world. Despite its obvious shortsightedness, the boast of Dobson and Barlow of Bolton in 1920 shows the considerable achievement made by the descendants of the first factory mechanics: 'It is just as safe to say, as of England's possessions, that the sun never sets on her machinery, which some country or another is running continuously the whole twenty-four hours.'

27

LEFT: *Platt Saco Lowell's rotor spinning machine. The fibres in the input sliver are separated by a small wire-covered cylinder and taken in an air stream into a rotating drum or rotor. Here they are thrown by centrifugal force into a channel cut around the rim of the rotor, where the fibres attach themselves to the end of the yarn being formed.*

BELOW: *A model of de Gennes's power loom. The specification of 1678 describes 'a new engine to make linen cloth without the aid of an artificer', but this first power loom was never produced commercially. As de Gennes's idea predates the invention of the fly shuttle it is interesting that the hand action of throwing the shuttle is reproduced mechanically by means of rapiers. The weft is carried in a small egg-shaped container by one rapier and is transferred in the centre of the shed to another which then withdraws. When the shed changes, the weft is similarly transferred back to the first rapier.*

One of the largest cylinder printing machines to be used in England. It was sited at the Turnbull and Stockdale printworks in Lancashire and was capable of printing designs with up to fourteen different colours in the repeat. Roller printing machines still produce the majority of Britain's printed fabric.

SPEED AND HIGH PRODUCTION

Some of the principal textile machinery inventions in the twentieth century have been developed by engineering firms not normally associated with textiles. Spinning machines and looms no longer emulate hand processes and this fresh approach has led to greater speeds and higher production.

The most expensive process in yarn production is spinning and great efforts have been made to achieve faster spindle speeds. Redesigned spindles and the use of mineral oil lubricants, allied to advanced engineering techniques, have achieved speeds of 15,000 rpm. The problem with virtually all traditional spinning processes is the need to impart twist by rotating the take-up package or bobbin with the spindle. Research has been aimed at systems which do not need to rotate the take-up package and has concentrated on the open-end system of spinning.

The most successful of these, *rotor spinning,* was first developed in Czechoslovakia in 1967 and rotor speeds have now reached 70,000 rpm, giving a production capability four times greater than the ring frame. At first open-end spinning was suitable only for short staple fibres and a limited range of counts (thickness of yarn). Some of these limitations have been overcome and trials continue using longer fibres and a wider count range. Another open-end system, air vortex spinning, is presently being developed and is likely to challenge rotor spinning in the future.

British textile machinery makers have generally tried to perfect traditional machines and many have gone out of business, unable to compete with modern systems. In 1931 a number of large textile engineering firms were amalgamated to form TMM (Textile Machinery Makers), controlled by Platts, and this company has remained at the forefront of spinning developments, producing its own high production system, which includes open-end spinning.

On the traditional loom the necessity of firing the shuttle at great speed across the loom from a static position, stopping it and reversing the process has limited the achievement of greater speed or efficiency. Research has been directed at developing 'shuttleless' looms which use various methods of weft insertion.

Dornier, the German aircraft manufacturers, started making textile machines in 1947 and produced their prototype *rapier loom* in 1963. The start-stop side-to-side operation of the shuttle is replaced by a sword stick or rapier which takes the weft thread through the warp sheet, deposits the yarn and moves back to its original position. Dornier has now developed tip to tip transfer using two rapiers inserted into the warp from either side of the loom simultaneously.

Sulzer Brothers, the Swiss locomotive makers, developed their weaving machine in the 1950s and its immense success has stemmed not only from its revolutionary weft insertion system but from the degree of precision engineering evident in all its working parts. These new looms cost many thousands of pounds each but are capable of producing cloth 12 feet (3.7 m) wide at 320 picks per minute.

A high level of weft insertion requires a fast changeover of shafts, which lift the warp threads. Development is concentrated on waved or multi-shed looms, where the warp threads are lifted in sections to accommodate the weft carrying projectile at the moment of its passage through the warp. In this manner a number of projectiles can enter the warp simultaneously.

The net result of twentieth-century developments has been the standardisation of yarns and fabrics produced in order to make full use of highly efficient automated systems.

Major developments have taken place in methods of fabric production, many new ideas coming from the knitting industry, but a revolutionary clothmaking technique, needlefelting, has taken over a large section of traditional woven fabric markets. In the fabric printing industry, greater use has been made of screen printing and more recently transfer printing for use on synthetic fabrics.

Microchip technology is being applied to textile design, with Jacquard computer systems, and it will soon be possible for a designer not familiar with computer technology to draw a design and have it converted into woven cloth within minutes.

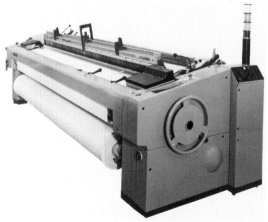

The Sulzer is a shuttleless loom utilising a number of tiny projectiles, 3½ inches (90 mm) long, with gripper attachments which are fired across the loom at tremendous speed by the reflex action of a torsion rod. Each projectile picks up the yarn from a large package or cone and takes it through the warp to where it is severed by a cutter motion. In the next cycle each loose end of weft is tucked in to give a strong selvedge while the projectiles travel on a conveyor under the warp back to a firing position. The high speed machine shown here is 11 feet 9¾ inches (3600 mm) wide and runs with a maximum weft insertion rate of 3609 feet (1100 metres) or 320 picks per minute.

GLOSSARY

Batting: the hand process of beating raw fibres with sticks, over a slatted table, in order to remove dirt and impurities.

Beat-up: the action of the reed in forcing the newly inserted weft thread into the body of cloth.

Carding: a process to clean and disentangle fibres and prepare them for spinning.

Combing: a process to straighten and parallelise longer fibres and remove shorter ones.

Cop: a cigar-shaped package of yarn.

Count: a measure of thickness of yarn.

Creel: a frame holding a number of bobbins of roving or yarn.

Dobby: a machine added to a loom which can be programmed to select and lift individual shafts carrying a number of warp threads.

Drafting, drawing out: thinning and lengthening a rope of fibres.

Faller wire: the device on a spinning mule or jenny which presents all the spun threads at right angles to the spindles for winding on.

Feeler motion: a device which detects an empty pirn and causes its replacement with a full weft pirn.

Fulling, milling: a process which deliberately uses the property of wool fibres to shrink to give a soft matted finish to woven woollen cloth.

Ginning: removing seeds from cotton fibres.

Going part: see *Sley*.

Hackling: a process similar to combing which removes shorter fibres (tow) from the long parallel flax fibres (line).

Healds: see *Shafts*.

Jacquard: a machine added to a loom which can be programmed to select and lift individual warp threads in order to create complex patterns.

Lap: a single layer of cotton fibres wound in sheet form round a roller.

Let-off: the rotation of the warp beam at the back of the loom, in order to release more warp for weaving.

Lofty: bulky, full and soft.

Milling: see *Fulling*.

Needlefelting: making cloth without spinning or weaving by consolidating layers of fibres.

Package: a cone, bobbin, or 'cheese' of roving or yarn.

Picker: normally a tough buffalo hide block which hits and propels the shuttle across the loom.

Picking: the act of firing the shuttle carrying the weft thread through the warp.

Pirn: a tube on which weft thread is wound, and which fits into a shuttle.

Quadrant: the device on a self-acting mule which regulates spindle speed.

Reed: a type of comb which keeps the warp threads in order and beats up the weft threads during weaving.

Roving, slubbing: a lightly twisted rope of fibres from which yarn is spun.

Screen printing: printing fabric by forcing dye through a fine mesh screen.

Shafts, healds: frames carrying warp threads.

Shedding: separating the warp threads in weaving to form a V-shaped passage so that the weft can be inserted.

Sley, going part: the frame which moves backwards and forwards to facilitate picking and beating up during weaving.

Sliver: an untwisted rope of fibres.

Slubbing: see *Roving*.

Staple length: average fibre length.

Stop motions: devices on a power loom which detect warp or weft thread breakages and cause the loom to stop.

Take-up: the method of winding woven cloth on to the cloth beam at the front of the loom.

Tin roller: a roller which runs the full length of the spinning machine and carries drive bands to each spindle.

Transfer printing: a dry printing process used on synthetic fabrics.

Trash: unwanted bits of seed, leaf, twig, etc, which need to be removed from bales of cotton.

Warp: the threads running lengthways in weaving.

Weft: in weaving, the threads going across the fabric.

PLACES TO VISIT

Intending visitors are advised to find out the times of opening before making a special journey.

UNITED KINGDOM

Bradford Industrial Museum, Moorside Road, Eccleshill, Bradford, West Yorkshire BD2 3HP. Telephone: Bradford (0274) 631756.

Coldharbour Mill Working Wool Museum, Coldharbour Mill, Uffculme, Cullompton, Devon EX15 3EE. Telephone: Cullompton (0884) 40960.

Greater Manchester Museum of Science and Industry, Liverpool Road, Castlefield, Manchester M3 4JP. Telephone: 061-832 2244.

Leeds Industrial Museum, Armley Mill, Canal Road, Armley, Leeds, West Yorkshire LS12 2QF. Telephone: Leeds (0532) 637862.

Lewis Museum of Textile Machinery, Exchange Street, Blackburn, Lancashire. Telephone: Blackburn (0254) 667130.

Museum of the Lancashire Textile Industry, Holcombe Road, Helmshore, Rossendale, Lancashire BB4 4NP. Telephone: Rossendale (0706) 226459.

Museum of the Woollen Industry, Drefach Felindre, Llandyssul, Dyfed. Telephone: Velindre (0559) 370453.

Paradise Mill, Old Park Lane, Macclesfield, Cheshire SK11 6TJ. Telephone: Macclesfield (0625) 618228.

Piece Hall Pre-industrial Museum and Art Gallery, Halifax, West Yorkshire. Telephone: Halifax (0422) 59031.

Quarry Bank Mill, Styal, Wilmslow, Cheshire SK9 4LA. Telephone: Wilmslow (0625) 527468.

Queen Street Mill, Queen Street, Harle Syke, Burnley, Lancashire. Telephone: Burnley (0282) 59996.

Science Museum, Exhibition Road, South Kensington, London SW7 2DD. Telephone: 01-589 3456.

Scottish Museum of Woollen Textiles, Tweedvale Mills, Walkerburn, Peebles EH43 6AH. Telephone: Walkerburn (089 687) 281 or 283.

Swansea Maritime and Industrial Museum, Museum Square, Maritime Quarter, Swansea, West Glamorgan. Telephone: Swansea (0792) 50351.

Tolson Memorial Museum, Ravensknowle Park, Wakefield Road, Huddersfield, West Yorkshire HD5 8DJ. Telephone: Huddersfield (0484) 30591 or 41455.

Tonge Moor Textile Museum, Tonge Moor Road, Bolton, Lancashire BL2 2LE. Telephone: Bolton (0204) 21394.

Ulster Museum, Botanic Gardens, Belfast BT9 5AB. Telephone: Belfast (0232) 668251-5.

Welsh Folk Museum, St Fagans, Cardiff CF5 6XB. Telephone: Cardiff (0222) 569441.

Wigan Pier, Wigan, Lancashire WN3 4EU. Telephone: Wigan (0942) 323666.

OTHER COUNTRIES

Museum Meiji Mura, I, Vichiyama Snuyama-ski, Aichi-ken, Japan.

Museum of American Textile History, 800 Massachusetts Avenue, North Andover, Massachusetts 01845, USA.

Museum of Industrial Archaeology and Textiles, Abrahamstraat 13, B9000 Ghent, Belgium.

National Museum of History and Technology, Smithsonian Institution, 14th Street and Constitution Avenue NW, Washington, DC 20560, USA.

Old Sturbridge Village, Sturbridge, Massachusetts 01566, USA.

Slater Mill Historic Site, Roosevelt Avenue, Pawtucket, Rhode Island 02865, USA.

Tekomuseum, Skaraborgsvägen 7, Boras, Sweden.

Twente and Gelder Textile Museum, Espoorstraat 182, 7511 CM Enschede, Overijssel, Holland.

ACKNOWLEDGEMENTS

Illustrations are acknowledged as follows: Armley Mills, Leeds Industrial Museum, page 3; Bolton Metropolitan Borough, Department of Education and Arts, cover; Bradford Industrial Museum, pages 24 (both), 25; International Institute for Cotton, page 29; Lancashire County Council, Museum of the Lancashire Textile Industry, pages 11 (all), 13, 14; Leeds City Art Galleries, page 5 (top); Lewis Museum of Textile Machinery, Blackburn, page 8 (top); Musée Historique des Tissus, Lyon, page 23; National Museum of Wales, Welsh Folk Museum, page 17 (top); Old Sturbridge Village, Massachusetts (photograph by Donald F. Eaton), page 9; Platt Saco Lowell UK Ltd, page 28 (top); Science Museum, London, pages 4 (bottom), 5 (bottom), 28 (bottom); Science Museum, London, Crown copyright, page 6; Smithsonian Institution, pages 17 (bottom), 19, 27; Sulzer UK Ltd, page 30; Ulster Museum, Belfast, page 18.